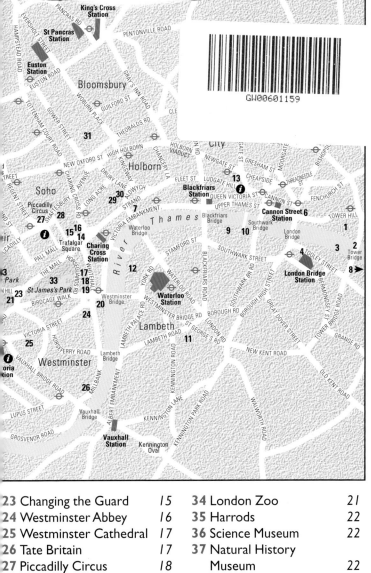

All information correct at time of going to press but may be subject to change.

3

Tower of London

This fortress was founded by William the Conqueror in 1078 to dominate and defend the city of London. It has been the scene of some of the bloodiest events in English history: kings and queens as well as traitors and spies have been murdered, executed, imprisoned or tortured within its walls.

⊖	Tower Hill
Bus:	RV1
Boat:	to Tower Pier from Westminster
Tel:	0870 756 6060
Open:	Mar–Oct: Mon–Sat 0900–1700, Sun 1000–1700; Nov–Feb: Tue–Sat 0900–1600, Sun–Mon 1000–1600

The oldest part is the central keep, known as the White Tower, which contains a collection of arms and armour. The Chapel of St John dates from 1080 and is the oldest church in London. The Crown Jewels are displayed in the Jewel House in Waterloo Barracks and include all the regalia used in the coronation ceremony and on state occasions. Yeoman warders – 'Beefeaters' – who assist today's visitors wear a distinctive uniform which dates from Tudor times.

Tower Bridge

⊖	Tower Hill
Bus:	42, 78, RV1
Boat:	to Tower Pier from Westminster
Tel:	020 7403 3761
Open:	Daily, Apr–Oct: 1000–1830 (last entry 1715), Nov–Mar: 0930–1800 (last entry 1645)

London's best known and most distinctive bridge has straddled the Thames for over a century. The twin drawbridges, which each weigh about 1,000 tonnes, take just 90 seconds to rise and are a working tribute to Victorian engineering genius. All the original machinery is used except that electric motors have replaced the steam engines. Walkways link the top of the towers and give superb views of the river.

HMS *Belfast*

HMS *Belfast* is a floating museum, saved from the scrapyard over 30 years ago. The 11,500-tonne cruiser which opened the bombardment of the Normandy coast on D-Day is now the most impressive of the many historic ships moored on the banks of the Thames. A tour of the ship includes the engine room, armaments, mess decks, punishment cells and operations rooms.

⊖	Tower Hill, London Bridge
Bus:	42, 78, RV1
Tel:	020 7940 6300
Open:	Daily, Mar–Oct: 1000–1800, Nov–Feb: 1000–1700 (last entry 1715/1615)

London Dungeon

⊖	London Bridge
Bus:	RV1
Tel:	020 7403 7221
Open:	Daily, 1000–1700, July–Aug: 1000–1900

In the dark vaults beneath London Bridge station is an exhibition of macabre events and horrors from London's past. The plague, executions and torture common in the Middle Ages are realistically recreated.

Museum of London

The Museum of London traces the life of London from prehistoric times to the modern day. The lifestyles of rich and poor are revealed in displays which include costumes, implements and exquisitely carved marble models. A popular exhibit is the Lord Mayor of London's decorated state coach, built in 1757 and still used every year for the Lord Mayor's Show, held in November.

⊖	Barbican, St Paul's
Bus:	56, 100
Tel:	0870 444 3850
Open:	Mon–Sat 1000–1750,
	Sun 1200–1750

The Monument

In 1666, the Great Fire of London raged for four days and devastated four-fifths of the buildings of the City of London. The Monument, designed by Sir Christopher Wren, was built in 1677 to commemorate the event. It is 61 metres (202 feet) high, which is exactly the distance separating the Monument from the Pudding Lane bakery where the fire began. The viewing area at the top of the column was enclosed after six people died by jumping from it – nearly as many as perished in the Great Fire itself.

⊖	Monument
Bus:	15, 25, N15
Tel:	020 7626 2717
Open:	Daily, 1000–1800

Somerset House

Designed by Sir William Chambers (1724–96), an advisor to King George III, Somerset House originally housed government offices. Now restored to its former splendour, it incorporates three museums: the Courtauld Institute Gallery with its collection of Impressionist paintings, Flemish and Italian Old Masters; the Gilbert Collection of decorative arts, and the Hermitage Rooms with displays from the State Hermitage Museum in St Petersburg.

⊖	Temple, Charing Cross, Embankment
Bus:	6, 9, 13, 23, 77A, RV1
Tel:	020 7845 4600
Open:	Daily, 1000–1800

Greenwich

At Greenwich, 5 miles downstream from London Bridge, is one of Sir Christopher Wren's architectural masterpieces – the Royal Naval College. The college, started in 1694 as a home for sailors, includes the magnificent Painted Hall. Behind the college is the Queen's House, now part of the National Maritime Museum, whose many galleries display its enormous maritime collection from 500 years of naval history. The Royal Observatory in Greenwich Park marks the prime meridian of zero longitude in the courtyard.

⇌	Cutty Sark (Docklands Light Railway), Greenwich or Maze Hill
Boat:	to Greenwich Pier from Westminster, Waterloo, or Tower Piers
National Maritime Museum	
Tel:	020 8312 6565
Open:	Daily, 1000–1700

Tate Modern

The redundant Bankside power station has been ingeniously converted into the Tate Modern art gallery. The collection includes works by such 20th-century masters as Picasso, Matisse, Dalí and Henry Moore, as well as a programme of changing exhibitions. A glass structure on top of the main building houses a restaurant with stunning views over London.

⊖	Southwark, London Bridge, Mansion House
Bus:	45, 63, 100, RV1
Tel:	020 7887 8888
Open:	Sun–Thu 1000–1800, Fri–Sat 1000–2200

Shakespeare's Globe

⊖	London Bridge, Southwark, Mansion House
Bus:	45, 63, 100, 344, 381, RV1
Tel:	020 7902 1400
Open:	Daily, 1000–1700

Shakespeare's Globe has been recreated close to the site of the original theatre erected on Bankside in 1599. It was constructed using traditional materials and building techniques from 400 years ago. Every summer plays by Shakespeare and his contemporaries are performed here in the open air.

Imperial War Museum

The Imperial War Museum is a record of conflicts fought by Britain and the Commonwealth during the 20th century. The collection includes aircraft, weapons, tanks, war paintings and artifacts of civilian life during wartime. Two 'experience' rooms recreate the sights and sounds of the trenches in World War I, and the Blitz of London during World War II.

⊖	Lambeth North, Elephant and Castle
Bus:	12, 53, 148, 344, 360, C10
Tel:	020 7416 5320
Open:	Daily, 1000–1800

	Waterloo, Westminster, Embankment
Bus:	76, 77, 211, 341, 381, 507

London Eye ticketline
Tel: 0870 990 8883
Open: Daily (except Christmas Day), Jul & Aug 0930–2200, June, Mon–Thu 0930–2100, Fri–Sun 0930–2200, May & Sep, Mon–Thu 0930–2000, Fri–Sun 0930–2100, Oct–Apr 0930–2000

Royal Festival Hall Box Office
Tel: 0871 663 2515

BFI IMAX Cinema
Tel: 0870 787 2525

London Aquarium
Tel: 020 7967 8000
Open: Daily, 1000–1800

▶ London Eye and the South Bank

One of the best ways to enjoy London is on the River Thames and the South Bank, between Westminster and Waterloo Bridges, offers a wide variety of attractions. On the river bank is London Eye – the highest viewing platform in London, taking passengers 137 metres (450 feet) above the River Thames. The Royal Festival Hall – London's main concert hall – the Hayward Gallery, the National Theatre and the BFI Centre form a cultural area, which includes the Southbank Centre. Nearby is the BFI IMAX cinema, which shows two and three-dimensional films on a massive screen. County Hall, once home to London's local government, now houses the London Aquarium and two art museums.

St Paul's Cathedral

St Paul's Cathedral rose out of the devastation of the Great Fire of London of 1666. The present baroque building is the fifth cathedral to be built on the site. The architect, Sir Christopher Wren, intended that the dome, which rises to 111 metres (365 feet), would be the cathedral's crowning glory. One of the two flanking towers contains a peal of 12 bells and the other houses the clock and Great Paul, the largest bell in England. St Paul's has been the setting for significant occasions in the nation's history, such as the funeral of the wartime leader, Sir Winston Churchill, the 25th anniversary of Queen Elizabeth II's reign, and the wedding of Prince Charles and the late Diana, Princess of Wales.

⊖	St Paul's, Mansion House, Blackfriars
Bus:	11, 15, 26, 76, 100, 172
Tel:	020 7236 4128
Open:	Mon–Sat 0830–1600, subject to special services

Trafalgar Square

From his vantage point 51 metres (167 feet) above the ground, Admiral Lord Nelson surveys Trafalgar Square, the memorial to his great naval victory in 1805. Today the Square is a popular venue for political rallies and tourists. The Admiral's statue looks towards the Houses of Parliament and is guarded by four magnificent bronze lions. In the north-east corner of the square stands the church of St Martin-in-the-Fields, a classical masterpiece by James Gibbs dating from 1721. It is well known today for its lunchtime recitals of classical music.

 Charing Cross, Embankment
Bus: 3, 6, 9, 11, 12, 24, 29, 139

National Gallery

 Charing Cross, Leicester Square
Bus: 3, 6, 9, 11, 12, 24, 29, 139
Tel: 020 7747 2423
Open: Daily, 1000–1800 (Wed until 2100)

Founded in 1834, the National Gallery houses one of the world's great art collections. It displays works of art representing every major master since the 15th century, including Leonardo da Vinci, Rubens, Caravaggio, Titian, Constable, Turner, Gainsborough, Monet, Holbein and Ingres.

National Portrait Gallery

The National Portrait Gallery collection numbers over 7,000 'faces' – paintings, sculptures, drawings, engravings and photographs – of the people who helped to shape British history, including Queen Elizabeth I, Sir Winston Churchill, William Shakespeare, Charles Dickens and Sir Christopher Wren.

 Charing Cross, Leicester Square
Bus: 3, 6, 9, 11, 12, 24, 29, 139
Tel: 020 7312 2463
Open: Sat–Wed 1000–1800, Thu–Fri 1000–2100

Horse Guards

Two mounted troopers of the Household Cavalry stand guard over the entrance to the Horse Guards. The low arch, guarded by two dismounted sentries, leads to Horse Guards Parade which is fringed by government offices and the Prime Minister's official Downing Street residence. The mounted troopers are on duty at their post in Horse Guards daily from 10 am to 4 pm. The colourful ceremony of Changing the Guard takes place at 11 am (10 am on Sundays).

⊖	Charing Cross
Bus:	3, 11, 12, 24, 53, 77A, 88, 148, 159, 211

Downing Street

No. 10 Downing Street is the official home of the British Prime Minister, No. 11, next door, that of the Chancellor of the Exchequer, and No. 12 is the office of the government's Chief Whip. Extensive renovations in the 20th century uncovered remains of the 16th-century palace of Whitehall, Roman pottery and the remains of a wooden Saxon hall. The gates recently erected at the entrance to Downing Street are a sombre reminder of the security measures now needed to protect public figures.

⊖	Westminster
Bus:	3, 11, 12, 24, 88, 148, 211

► Cabinet War Rooms

	Westminster
Bus:	3, 11, 12, 24, 88, 148, 211
Tel:	020 7839 4906
Open:	Daily, Apr–Sep: 0930–1800, Oct–Mar: 1000–1800 (last admission 1715)

Deep under the heart of London can be found the entrance, at the end of King Charles Street, to the Churchill Museum and Cabinet War Rooms. During World War II, this warren of rooms was used by Sir Winston Churchill, the War Cabinet and the Chiefs of Staff.

► Houses of Parliament

At Westminster, on the bank of the Thames, are the Houses of Parliament where laws governing British life are debated and enacted. Built in 1840 after a fire destroyed the previous building, and officially known as the Palace of Westminster, the complex includes the House of Commons, the House of Lords, Westminster Hall, and the 98-metre (320-foot) high Clock Tower. This famous landmark contains the bell known as Big Ben. Westminster Hall, the great hall of the royal palace, dates from

	Westminster, St James's Park
Bus:	3, 11, 12, 24, 88, 148, 211
No general public admission	

medieval times. Outside stands a statue to Oliver Cromwell, who established the supremacy of parliament over the monarchy in the 17th century.

▶ Buckingham Palace

Buckingham Palace, the best-known royal palace in the world, was built in 1703 and bought 60 years later by King George III. His extravagant but stylish son, King George IV, commissioned John Nash, the court architect, to remodel it in 1821. In 1847 Queen Victoria added an east wing, which was changed in 1913 to the present stern but dignified classical façade.

The Royal Standard flutters over the east front when Her Majesty the Queen is in residence. Opposite, at the head of the Mall, is the Queen Victoria Memorial. The statue represents the ideals of motherhood, truth, justice, peace and progress. The State Rooms are used to receive visiting heads of state and for investiture ceremonies where Her Majesty and other members of the Royal Family bestow titles, honours and awards for outstanding service.

	St James's Park, Victoria, Hyde Park Corner
Bus:	2, 11, 24, 148, 211, 507
Tel:	020 7766 7300
Open:	Daily, Aug–Sep: 0930–1630 (last entry 1515); ticket office opens 0900 and closes when the last ticket has been sold. Visitors are advised to buy their ticket before midday

▶ Royal Mews

Built by John Nash in 1826, the Royal Mews form a quadrangle where the processional horses are stabled and coaches in the Royal Collection are displayed. The magnificent coaches include the Gold State Coach used for coronations, the Irish State Coach used for the State Opening of Parliament and the Glass State Coach used for royal weddings.

	Victoria, St James's Park
Bus:	2, 11, 24, 36, 73
Tel:	020 7766 7302
Open:	Sat–Thu 1100–1600; daily 1000–1700 during Buckingham Palace summer opening

▶ Changing the Guard

Buckingham Palace is guarded by the five regiments of Foot Guards, easily recognised by their scarlet uniforms and bearskins. The Guard is changed in a colourful display of military pageantry and precision. The Queen's Guard, accompanied by a band, marches from Wellington Barracks into the Palace forecourt, where there is a symbolic transfer of command. The ceremony starts at 11.15 and lasts about an hour.

⊖	St James's Park, Victoria, Hyde Park Corner, Green Park
Bus:	2, 11, 24, 148, 211, 507
Tel:	020 7766 7300

The Guard is changed daily from April to June, and every other day for the rest of the year

▶ Westminster Abbey

No church in Britain has been so closely connected with the Crown and the nation's history as Westminster Abbey. Coronations of every king or queen (except two) spanning 900 years have been held here. The present Abbey was founded in the 11th century by King Edward the Confessor, on the site of an earlier place of worship. The Chapel of the Pyx (currently closed) and the Undercroft which now houses the Abbey's museum, are 11th century but most of this magnificent Gothic building dates from the 13th and 14th centuries. The twin west towers were added in the 18th century.

St Edward the Confessor's chapel, the most sacred part of the Abbey, is the burial place of kings, while the sanctuary is the setting for coronations. The 13th-century Chapter House, an octagonal chamber 18 metres (60 feet) across, is sometimes called the 'cradle of all free parliaments', as it was parliament's meeting place from the 14th to 16th centuries.

⊖	Westminster, St James's Park
Bus:	3, 11, 12, 24, 88, 148, 211
Tel:	020 7654 4900
Open:	Mon–Fri 0930–1545, except Wed 0930–1800; Sat 0930–1345;
Chapter House & Museum	
Tel:	020 7654 4832
Open:	Daily, 1030–1600

Westminster Cathedral

Westminster Cathedral is the leading Roman Catholic church in England. Its striking exterior uses 12 million red bricks and white Portland stone in a striped Byzantine style, which not everyone appreciated when it was completed in 1903. The cathedral has a campanile (St Edward's Tower), 83 metres (273 feet) high. Saucer domes cover the 18-metre (60-foot) wide nave – the widest nave in England – which can hold a congregation of 2,000. Eric Gill's carved limestone bas-reliefs of the Stations of the Cross are considered an outstanding modern work of art. Treasures include some preserved fragments of the True Cross and a mitre of St Thomas Becket.

⊖	Victoria, St James's Park
Bus:	11, 24, 148, 211, 507
Tel:	020 7798 9055/020 7798 9097 (for times of Mass)
Open:	Mon–Sat 0800–1900, Sun 0800–1700

Tate Britain

Built on the site of the old Millbank prison, Tate Britain contains the national collection of British art. The gallery houses many masterpieces, including well-known portraits by Reynolds and Gainsborough, Constable landscapes and major works by the Pre-Raphaelites. The largest collection of oils, water-colours and sketches by Turner are displayed in the Clore Gallery, a separate wing dedicated to this great artist.

⊖	Westminster, Victoria, Pimlico
Bus:	2, 24, 36, 77A, 88, 185, C10
Tel:	020 7887 8888
Open:	Daily, 1000–1750

Piccadilly Circus

Piccadilly Circus – at the junction of five busy streets – has long been a famous London landmark. In the centre, over a fountain, is the statue popularly called Eros, the Greek god of love, but in fact designed in the 19th century as a symbol of Christian charity – a monument to Lord Shaftesbury, a philanthropist. The name Piccadilly was coined by a 17th-century dressmaker who lived in the area and who created a frilled collar called a 'piccadil'.

⊖	Piccadilly Circus
Bus:	3, 6, 9, 12, 14, 15, 19, 22, 38

Trocadero, Piccadilly

⊖	Piccadilly Circus, Leicester Square
Bus:	3, 6, 9, 12, 14, 15, 19, 22, 38, 88, 159
Trocadero	
Tel:	09068 88 11 00
Open:	Fri & Sat, 1000–0100, Sun–Thu 1000–0000
Funland	
Tel:	020 7292 3642
Open:	see above

Piccadilly has been a centre of entertainment for over a century. The Trocadero, built behind a former music hall façade, is home to a variety of 21st-century restaurants, shops and entertainment facilities designed to amuse and delight. Within the Trocadero is Funland, one of the world's largest indoor entertainment centres. Attractions include ten-pin bowling, a sports bar, American pool, and simulator rides and games, including dodgems.

18

Seven hundred years ago this area was a 'convent garden' supplying fruit and vegetables to Westminster Abbey. In the 17th century, Inigo Jones designed London's first elegant square here, but, by the 18th century, Covent Garden was again a market supplying fruit, vegetables and flowers. In the 1970s the market moved elsewhere and the renovated market building became the centrepiece of this fashionable area, with interesting shops, craft markets, bars and cafés. Also in the square are St Paul's Church, whose portico acts as an open-air stage for buskers and entertainers, the London Transport Museum and a Theatre Museum.

	Covent Garden
Bus:	6, 9, 13, 15, 23, 77A, RV1

London Transport Museum

	Covent Garden
Bus:	6, 9, 13, 15, 23, 77A, RV1
Tel:	020 7565 7299
Open:	Sat–Thu 1000–1800, Fri 1100–1800

The London Transport Museum houses a collection of historic buses, trams, underground trains and posters. It focuses on themes such as art and design, suburbia, the travel revolution, the Victorian era and wartime.

British Museum

The British Museum is regarded as one of the world's leading museums. Its treasures include the Elgin Marbles, the superb Greek sculptures which once adorned the Parthenon in Athens; the Rosetta Stone, which helped scholars decipher Egyptian hieroglyphics; the Roman silver cache which forms the Mildenhall Treasure, and a superb selection of Egyptian mummies. The British Library once shared this classical colonnaded building, but is now next to St Pancras Station.

⊖	Tottenham Court Road, Goodge Street, Holborn, Russell Square
Bus:	7, 10, 24, 29, 73, 134
Tel:	020 7323 8299
Open:	Sat–Wed 1000–1730, Thu–Fri 1000–2030

Madame Tussaud's and the Stardome

Marie Tussaud exhibited her waxworks of the victims of the French Revolution in Paris in 1789. They were so popular she opened a museum in London in 1835. Today's exhibition contains fascinating likenesses of the Royal Family, international statesmen, explorers, popular entertainers, film stars, and sportsmen. Tableaux of famous crimes are shown in the Chamber of Horrors.

Next door, the Stardome presents The Wonderful World of Stars. Created by award-winning Aardman Animations it transforms the dome into a spectacular show of stars – the celebrity variety.

⊖	Baker Street
Bus:	18, 27, 30, 205, 453
Tel:	Ticketline 0870 999 0293
	Madame Tussaud's
Open:	Sat & Sun 0900–1800, Mon–Fri 0930–1730

The Royal Parks

London's royal parks, once the private preserve of the nation's monarch, are now open for all to enjoy. St James's, in front of Buckingham Palace, is considered the most beautiful. Hyde Park is linked to Kensington Gardens by the Serpentine Lake and together form the largest open space in central London. Regent's Park was designed in 1812 by John Nash and named after the stylish Prince Regent (later King George IV). Within the Inner Circle is the pretty Queen Mary Gardens and an open-air theatre.

	St James's Park, Hyde Park Corner, Marble Arch, Knightsbridge, High Street Kensington, Lancaster Gate, Queensway, Bayswater, Regent's Park, Camden Town
Bus:	10, 11, 12, 24, 27, 74, N27
Open:	Hyde Park, St James's Park, Kensington Gardens and Regent's Park are open daily, the gates are closed at dusk and the parks at midnight

London Zoo

London Zoo, in the north-east corner of Regent's Park, is one of the world's oldest and most important zoos. Here you can see over 12,000 animals from all over the world. The emphasis is on education and conservation, and there is a wide-ranging breeding programme for endangered species.

	Camden Town
Bus:	274, N274
Tel:	020 7722 3333
Open:	Mar–Oct: 1000–1730, Nov–Feb: 1000–1600

► Harrods

Harrods in Knightsbridge is London's best-known store. The store began as a small grocer's shop in 1849 but by 1894, Henry Harrod, the founder's son, claimed to 'serve the world' – it has even delivered an elephant to Ronald Reagan! Harrod's was the first store in the world to install an escalator, but Victorian customers were so overcome by riding the 'moving staircase' that attendants were posted at the top to administer brandy to gentlemen and smelling salts to ladies. The interior of the present building includes Art Nouveau and Art Deco styles.

⊖	Knightsbridge
Bus:	9, 10, 14, 52, 74, 414, C1, N74
Tel:	020 7730 1234
Open:	Mon–Sat 1000–1900

► Science Museum

Prince Albert, consort to Queen Victoria, was the inspiration behind the establishment of several museums in South Kensington. The Science Museum, founded in 1856, covers all aspects of science and engineering, with many hands-on exhibits which appeal to children. It includes transport – everything from road and rail to air and space – steam engines, electric turbines, nuclear physics, medical equipment, and even Napoleon's toothbrush!

⊖	South Kensington
Bus:	49, 70, 74, C1
Tel:	0870 870 4868
Open:	Daily, 1000–1800

► Natural History Museum

The exterior of the Natural History Museum is faced with finely carved animals. Inside, the collection runs to some 50 million items, the most popular being reconstructed dinosaurs – diplodocus, triceratops and tyrannosaurus.

⊖	South Kensington
Bus:	49, 70, 74, C1
Tel:	020 7942 5725
Open:	Daily 1000–1750

► Victoria and Albert Museum

The museum collects fine and applied art from many countries. Treasures include carved ivories, musical instruments, tapestries, miniatures, sculptures, furniture, and costumes. Among the noted exhibits are the Raphael Cartoons, commissioned for the Sistine Chapel in the Vatican, and the Canning Jewel, depicting a merman in gold and jewels.

⊖	South Kensington
Bus:	14, 49, 70, 74, C1
Tel:	020 7942 2000
Open:	Sat–Thu 1000–1745, Fri 1000–2200